SOUTH CAROLINA

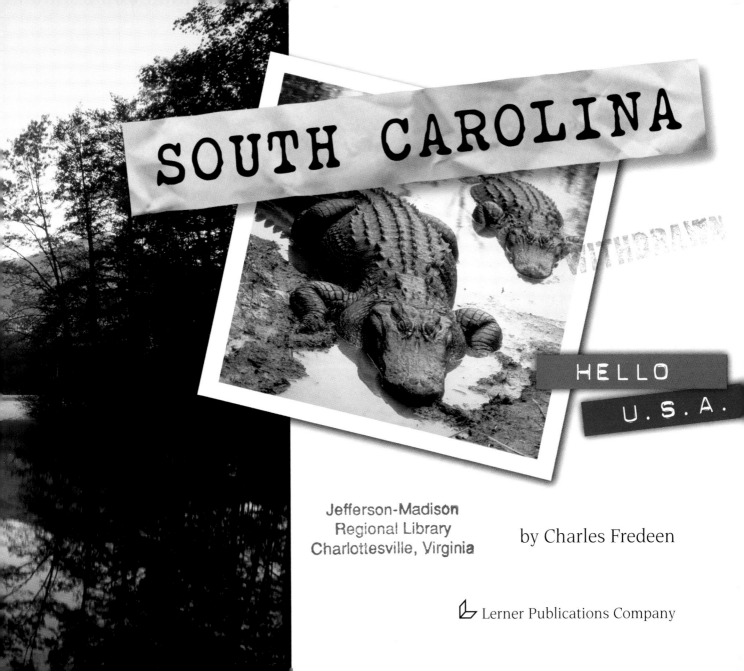

# SOUTH CAROLINA

HELLO
U.S.A.

by Charles Fredeen

Lerner Publications Company

*You'll find this picture of palmetto leaves at the beginning of each chapter in this book. South Carolinians enjoy palmetto leaf buds in salads and use them to make pickles and relishes. The palmetto appears on South Carolina's state flag and its state seal. It represents a fort built of palmetto logs on Sullivan's Island. In 1776 American forces defeated the British navy at the fort.*

Cover (left): Palm trees outside a Charleston mansion.  Cover (right): Venus's-flytrap. Pages 2–3: Table Rock State Park.  Page 3: Alligators at Myrtle Beach.

*This book is available in two editions:*
Library binding by Lerner Publications Company, a division of Lerner Publishing Group
Soft cover by First Avenue Editions, an imprint of Lerner Publishing Group
241 First Avenue North
Minneapolis, MN 55401 U.S.A.

Website address: www.lernerbooks.com


Library of Congress Cataloging-in-Publication Data

Fredeen, Charles, 1956–
    South Carolina / by Charles Fredeen. (Rev. and expanded 2nd ed.)
        p.   cm. — (Hello U.S.A.)
    Includes index.
    Summary: An introduction to the land, history, people, economy, and environment of South Carolina.
    ISBN: 0–8225–4087–8 (lib. bdg. : alk. paper)
    ISBN: 0–8225–0794–3 (pbk. : alk. paper)
    1. South Carolina—Juvenile literature. [1. South Carolina.] I. Title. II. Series.
F269.3 .F74 2002
975.7—dc21                                                              2001006407

Manufactured in the United States of America
1 2 3 4 5 6 – JR – 07 06 05 04 03 02

# CONTENTS

A great blue heron hunts for dinner on South Carolina's Atlantic coast.

# THE LAND

## The Palmetto State

outh Carolina, located in the southeastern United States, has a varied and beautiful landscape. The eastern part of the state borders the Atlantic Ocean. The western part of the state is filled with hills, forests, and mountains. Thousands of years ago, Indians made their homes here. Later, during the Revolutionary War, South Carolina was the site of many important battles. The state played a big role during the Civil War, too. Modern-day South Carolina has a diverse economy. Farming, manufacturing, and tourism provide jobs for many South Carolina residents.

Oaks are one of the many kinds of trees found in South Carolina.

Kings Mountain
National Military Park

Chesnee
Cowpens
Blacksburg
Springfield
Gaffney
Salem
Greenville
Cowpens
National
Battlefield
Rock Hill

Greenwood

Darlington

★ **Columbia**

Sumter

Myrtle
Beach

Salley

Georgetown

N
W E
S

North
Charleston

Cape Romain
National Wildlife Refuge

Charleston

Fort Sumter
National Monument

Beaufort

The drawing of South Carolina on this
page is called a political map. It shows
features created by people, including cities,
railways, and parks. The map on the facing
page is called a physical map. It shows
physical features of South Carolina, such as
coasts, islands, mountains, rivers, and lakes. The
colors represent a range of elevations, or heights
above sea level (see legend box). This map also
shows the geographical regions of South Carolina.

## SOUTH CAROLINA
## Political Map

★  State capital

0        15        30 Miles

0    15    30    45    60 Kilometers

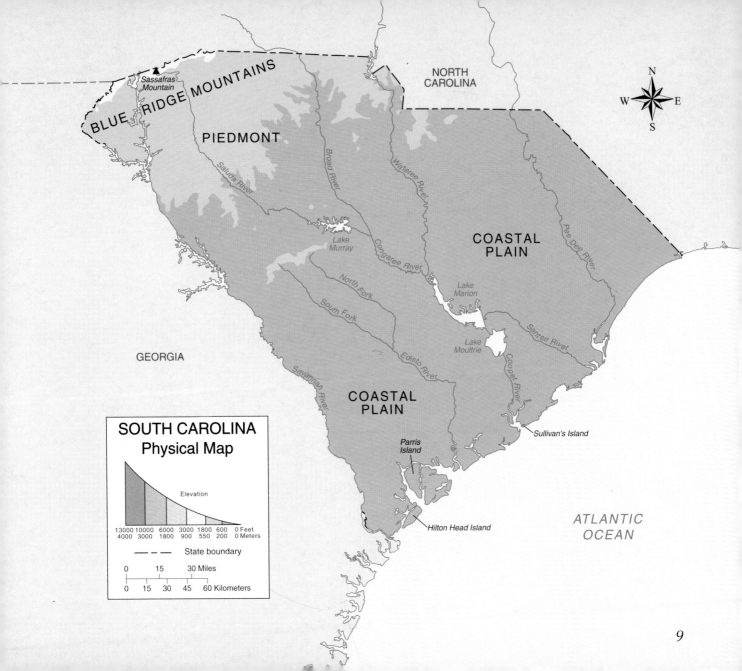

**SOUTH CAROLINA**
Physical Map

BLUE RIDGE MOUNTAINS

Sassafras
Mountain

PIEDMONT

GEORGIA

NORTH
CAROLINA

COASTAL
PLAIN

Saluda River

Broad River

Wateree River

Pee Dee River

Lake
Murray

Congaree River

North Fork

South Fork

Lake
Marion

Lake
Moultrie

Santee River

Cooper River

Edisto River

Savannah River

COASTAL
PLAIN

Parris
Island

Hilton Head Island

Sullivan's Island

ATLANTIC
OCEAN

Elevation

13000 10000 6000 3000 1800 600 0 Feet
4000 3000 1800 900 550 200 0 Meters

- - - State boundary

0    15    30 Miles

0  15  30  45  60 Kilometers

N
W    E
S

South Carolina is divided into three land regions: the Coastal Plain, the Piedmont, and the Blue Ridge Mountains. The Coastal Plain is also called the Low Country because it is so close to sea level. The Piedmont and the Blue Ridge Mountains together are called the Up Country because they rise higher than the Coastal Plain.

The Coastal Plain covers the southeastern half of South Carolina. Thousands of years ago, the Atlantic Ocean swelled over most of the low-lying plain. When the ocean pulled back to its present shoreline, it left the sandy soil that blankets the Coastal Plain.

The low, flat part of the Coastal Plain stretches inland past the **swamps,** or wetlands, that soak much of the Low Country. To the northwest, the plain rises into rolling hills of sand that are covered with pine forests.

The Blue Ridge Mountains stretch along South Carolina's northwestern edge.

At the Fall Line, waterfalls tumble down into the Low Country.

The sand hills of the Coastal Plain divide the region from the Piedmont, a higher, rockier region that covers most of northwestern South Carolina. The Piedmont's forested hills slope down toward the Coastal Plain. As the rivers of the rocky Up Country tumble down onto the sandy Low Country, they form a series of waterfalls called the Fall Line.

The Blue Ridge Mountains pass through a tiny sliver of land along South Carolina's northwestern border. Pine-covered peaks stand out among the rolling hills and valleys of the Blue Ridge. Sassafras Mountain, the state's highest point, overlooks this region.

Several rivers run across South Carolina. The Santee River and its major branches—the Wateree and the Congaree—divide the state in half. In eastern South Carolina, the Pee Dee River enters the state near the Fall Line. The Savannah River marks the border between South Carolina and Georgia. Other rivers include the Edisto, the Broad, and the Saluda.

Many dams have been built on the state's rivers.

The dams collect water for **hydropower,** or water-power. When released, the water turns wheels that generate electricity for use in homes and businesses. Water held back by the dams also creates most of South Carolina's lakes, including Lake Marion, the biggest.

Hot, sticky summers and mild winters are typical of South Carolina's climate. July temperatures hover around 80° F on the coast, but the mountains are usually cooler. In winter the Blue Ridge Mountains block cold air from the northwest, keeping temperatures in the state well above freezing.

Rainfall is plentiful in most parts of South Carolina, with an average of 48 inches measured each year. Snow rarely falls except in the mountains, which get more moisture overall than the rest of the state. Tornadoes and hurricanes sometimes threaten South Carolina's people, cities, and land.

Hurricane Hugo and other fierce storms have caused destruction along the South Carolina coast.

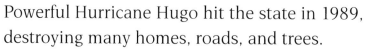

Powerful Hurricane Hugo hit the state in 1989, destroying many homes, roads, and trees.

Forests cover much of South Carolina. Pines, tulip trees, cottonwoods, and magnolias grow throughout the state. Webs of Spanish moss, a flowering plant with no roots, hang from cypress and live oak trees. South Carolina gets its nickname, the Palmetto State, from the many palmetto trees that grow here.

Azaleas and laurels brighten the South Carolina countryside in the spring. And insects should be wary here. South Carolina is one of only two states where Venus's-flytraps, bug-eating plants, grow wild. (They also grow in North Carolina.)

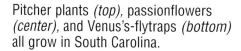

Pitcher plants *(top)*, passionflowers *(center)*, and Venus's-flytraps *(bottom)* all grow in South Carolina.

The swamps of the Coastal Plain shelter many alligators and a few black bears.  The region also hosts flocks of ducks and geese during the winter.  Clams, crabs, and shrimp live just off the coast in the Atlantic Ocean.  Plenty of white-tailed deer bound through the forests of the Piedmont and the Blue Ridge Mountains, sharing the woods with opossums, rabbits, raccoons, and wildcats.

South Carolina's swamps are home to many alligators.

## Natives and Newcomers

 outh Carolina was named for King Charles I of Great Britain. (*Carolina* comes from the Latin word for "Charles.") But the state's story begins long before the king's reign.

Thousands of years ago, more than 25 different Native American, or Indian, groups lived in the hills and lowlands of South Carolina. Most of the groups lived in villages. For food, the Indians grew crops, fished, and hunted wild game.

English colonists named the Carolinas for King Charles I.

Long before Europeans came to South Carolina, Indians built homes, farms, and villages there.

Monuments throughout the state honor the Catawba and other Indians.

By the 1500s, one of the largest Indian nations was the Catawba, a powerful group that built its villages near the Wateree River. The Catawba grew corn, squash, beans, and gourds. When the Indians needed meat, they hunted deer or fished the rivers.

The Cherokee, another large and powerful nation, lived in South Carolina's Up Country. Like the Catawba, the Cherokee built villages along rivers and streams. The Cherokee grew a lot of maize, or corn. They cooked maize by roasting or boiling it. The Cherokee also gathered crab apples, cherries, chestnuts, and other wild plant foods.

Some of these Indians may have met Europeans for the first time in 1521. That year, a group of Spaniards explored the Carolina coast. Forty years later, French explorers tried to settle in the same area. Plagued by hunger and disease, both European groups returned to their homelands shortly after arriving.

Cherokee hunters covered themselves with deerskins. This disguise made it easier for the hunters to approach and shoot living deer.

Great Britain was the next European country to take an interest in the Carolina coast. In the early 1600s, Great Britain claimed territory in North America that would later become South Carolina, North Carolina, and Georgia. Fifty years later, in 1663, King Charles II of Britain gave this territory, called Carolina, to eight wealthy British men. These men paid people from Great Britain to move to Carolina and start a **colony,** or settlement.

Under King Charles II, Britain built the first permanent settlement in South Carolina.

In Britain the settlers loaded up their ships with food and other necessities. Their cargo included three Africans, who were among the earliest black slaves in the South. The settlers arrived in 1670 and built South Carolina's first permanent colony at Albemarle Point, near modern-day Charleston.

The British colonists soon angered several of South Carolina's Indian nations. White traders, who

When the British arrived at Albemarle Point, they met the Indians who already lived there.

bought thousands of deerskins from the Indians each year, often treated the Native Americans poorly. Traders kidnapped hundreds of Indian women and children and forced them to become slaves. The traders then killed Indian men who tried to save their families.

When the colonists built a new town on land that belonged to the Yamasee Indians, the Yamasee grew angry. They attacked white settlements, killing 90 settlers and traders. Fifteen other Indian nations, including the powerful Catawba, fought alongside the Yamasee in the war that followed. It ended less than two years later, when an army of white settlers drove the Yamasee south into Florida.

Settlers and Indians clashed during the Yamasee War. Eventually, the Indian nations were defeated.

Many Indians died in the Yamasee War. But these losses soon seemed small compared to the number of Indians who died from diseases brought by the Europeans. Eventually, only small groups of Indians were left in the region.

# Stede Bonnet

Pirates were a constant threat to ships sailing in and out of Charleston Harbor in the early 1700s. In 1718 South Carolinians finally captured one of the most wicked villains—Stede Bonnet.

Bonnet and his crew had sailed into a hiding place along the Carolina coast one night. The governor of South Carolina learned that Bonnet lurked outside the colony and sent Colonel William Rhett to capture the outlaw.

Rhett soon found the pirates. As Bonnet tried to escape, Rhett sailed after him until both ships suddenly ground to a halt. Bonnet and Rhett were stuck on a sandbar.

The men waited five hours for the ocean tide to rise. The force of the tide soon freed Rhett's ship. The pirates, still stuck, surrendered in fright.

Rhett brought the captives back to Charleston. Twenty-nine members of Bonnet's crew were hanged. Bonnet escaped but was recaptured. He was hanged one month after the rest of his gang.

In the early 1700s, Great Britain divided Carolina into new colonies. The northern portion became North Carolina. Georgia was set up in the south, leaving South Carolina in between. South Carolina was one of 13 British colonies in North America. To increase the colony's population, South Carolina welcomed immigrants from Germany, Ireland, and other European countries.

By the 1700s, Charleston was an important port city. Ships sailed in and out of the harbor, carrying goods and travelers to and from Europe and other cities in North America.

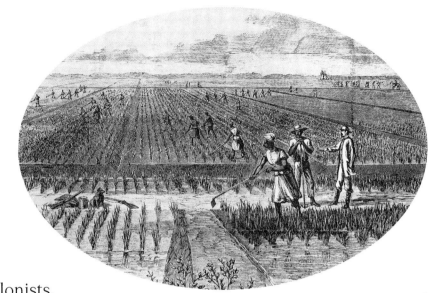

Slaves tended to rice and other crops on big plantations in the Low Country.

The state's first colonists, who lived in the Low Country, had come mostly from Britain. They earned their money by growing crops such as rice and indigo (a source of blue dye) on plantations, or large farms. They used African slaves to work the plantations. The later immigrants settled mostly in the Up Country. Unlike the earlier settlers, they came from many countries, each with different customs. Most of these new settlers owned small farms, so they didn't use slaves.

The Battle of Kings Mountain was an important victory for the American colonists.

As more settlers came to South Carolina, the British king forced them to pay new taxes and to follow new laws. Although South Carolinians disagreed on many things, most of them agreed that the king had no right to make them pay these taxes.

In 1775 South Carolina joined the 12 other colonies in a fight for their independence from Britain. This fight became known as the American Revolution.

During the Revolution, which lasted eight years, 137 battles were fought in South Carolina—more than in any other colony. In 1781 colonial soldiers forced the British army out of South Carolina. By 1783 Britain had lost the war, and the colonists formed their own country—the United States of America. South Carolina joined the Union in 1788, becoming the new country's eighth state.

General Francis Marion *(second from right)* and his soldiers hid in swamps and made surprise attacks on British troops.

After the war, an inventor named Eli Whitney built the cotton gin. This machine pulled cottonseed 50 times faster than people could. Cotton soon became South Carolina's most important crop. As cotton plantations grew, South Carolina's planters depended more heavily on slave labor to pick cotton from the fields.

Like people in other Southern states, South Carolinians bought slaves from Africa. With the rise

With the invention of the cotton gin, the cotton industry boomed in South Carolina. Much of the cotton was shipped to Great Britain.

of the cotton industry, planters bought even more slaves. Soon, more slaves than free people lived in the state. White planters began to worry that slaves might organize an uprising. If they did, the outnumbered planters could lose all their power and property.

South Carolinians also worried that the U.S. government was paying more attention to the concerns of Northerners than to those of Southerners. Unlike the South, where crops were the greatest money-makers, the North earned much of its money from manufactured goods. The U.S. government wanted to make sure that Americans bought the products made in Northern factories.

To do this, the government raised the **tariffs,** or fees, it charged on goods bought from other countries. The tariffs made foreign products more expensive to buy. Because South Carolina's planters depended on trade with Britain, they began to lose money when they traded their cotton for British goods.

For the next several decades, the North and South had many clashes, especially about slavery. Many Northerners thought slavery was cruel and should be outlawed. Many Southerners disagreed. Abraham Lincoln, a Northerner, was elected president of the United States in 1860. The white people of the South feared

South Carolinian John C. Calhoun *(pointing)* held several national offices, including congressman and vice president. He argued against tariff laws that hurt Southern states.

Plantation owners attended auctions where men, women, and children were bought and sold as slaves.

Lincoln would use his power to rid the South of slavery, which could lead Southerners into poverty.

Partly to protect itself from financial ruin, South Carolina decided to **secede** (withdraw) from the United States. Ten other Southern states followed South Carolina. The eleven former states formed their own country—the Confederate States of America. Soon, the United States and the Confederate States were at war.

Confederate troops attacked Fort Sumter in Charleston Harbor, marking the start of the Civil War.

The first shots of the Civil War were fired on April 12, 1861, when Confederate troops fired at Fort Sumter, a Union fort in South Carolina's Charleston Harbor. Thirty-five hours later, the outnumbered Northern troops were defeated. Despite all the exploding shells, there was only one death in the battle—a horse.

About 600,000 soldiers, however, would die during the next four years of the Civil War. More than 10,000 South Carolinians lost their lives in fierce and bloody battles before the South surrendered to the North in 1865.

Union troops invaded South Carolina and burned the city of Columbia in 1865.

After the Civil War, South Carolinians began rebuilding damaged cities, such as Columbia.

The Civil War left much of South Carolina in ruins. Its capital city, Columbia, had been burned to the ground by Union troops. Other cities, homes, plantations, and crops had been destroyed throughout the state.

President Lincoln had freed the slaves, but most of them had no money, no homes, and no jobs. They could not even afford to move to the North, where there were more jobs. Many black families became **sharecroppers,** farming another person's land and receiving a small share of the crops they grew as payment for their labor.

For the next 12 years, Union soldiers lived in South Carolina to oversee **Reconstruction,** or the rebuilding of the South. In 1868 a new state constitution gave black men the right to vote. The U.S. government then allowed South Carolina to rejoin the United States.

South Carolina recovered slowly from the Civil War. Some planters started growing cotton again, but many farmers couldn't afford to hire former slaves or to rebuild their farms.

Wade Hampton *(lifting hat)* was elected governor of South Carolina in 1876 and 1878. He later served as a U.S. senator.

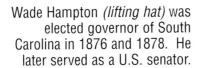

35

Thousands of South Carolinians took jobs in textile mills in the late 1800s. Because many families were poor, even children had to work.

They turned instead to manufacturing. In the Up Country, mills were built to make textiles, or cloth. Workers earned only 72 cents a day, but people welcomed any job they could find.

The state's growing textile industry did not help black people. Most mills refused to give jobs to African Americans. In the late 1800s, lawmakers passed what became known as **Jim Crow laws.** These laws said that black people couldn't use schools, hospitals, drinking fountains, rest rooms, hotels, or restaurants that were used by white people.

Black people could not change these laws because white lawmakers had found ways to prevent African Americans from voting. Many black people left South Carolina and moved to Northern cities, where they hoped they would have better opportunities.

By law, whites and blacks could not use the same drinking fountains in South Carolina. Unfair laws were not changed until the 1950s and 1960s.

From the 1940s to the 1960s, African Americans throughout the country joined the **civil rights movement,** fighting to end the Jim Crow laws and to win equal voting rights.

During the same period, factories spread throughout South Carolina. Manufacturing became more important than agriculture. As the state began to make more money from manufacturing, it also began to pay attention to the issues of the civil rights movement.

South Carolinans have learned to embrace the racial and cultural diversity of their state.

Since 1970, factories and offices in South Carolina have been opening their doors to black workers. Progress has been made toward the goal of equal rights. White students and African American students sit side by side in South Carolina's classrooms. In 1983, I. DeQuincey Newman became South Carolina's first black state senator since Reconstruction.

In the 1990s, many African Americans spoke out about the South Carolina government. They were angry because the Confederate flag, the banner of the Confederate States of America, still flew over the South Carolina statehouse. Many African Americans saw the flag as a symbol of slavery and racism. Many white South Carolinians, on the other hand, saw the flag as a symbol of pride in their Southern heritage.

In July 2000, the government made a compromise. The flag was lowered from over the statehouse. It was moved to an area near the statehouse, in front of a memorial to Confederate soldiers. Some African Americans were unhappy with the compromise. They thought the flag should be removed from government property altogether. Other people thought that the compromise would help heal racial divisions and help South Carolina move toward a more harmonious future.

# PEOPLE & ECONOMY

## A Rich Heritage

he differences between South Carolina's black people and white people and between the Up Country and the Low Country are no longer as great as they once were. Whether in cotton fields, textile mills, or government offices, South Carolina's 4 million residents are working together.

More than half of South Carolina's people live in cities. Columbia, the state's capital and largest city, sprawls along the border between the Low Country and the Up Country. Charleston, full of old gardens and mansions, is the second largest city. North Charleston and Greenville are the only other cities that have more than 50,000 people.

Beachgoers in Myrtle Beach, a city on South Carolina's Atlantic coast.

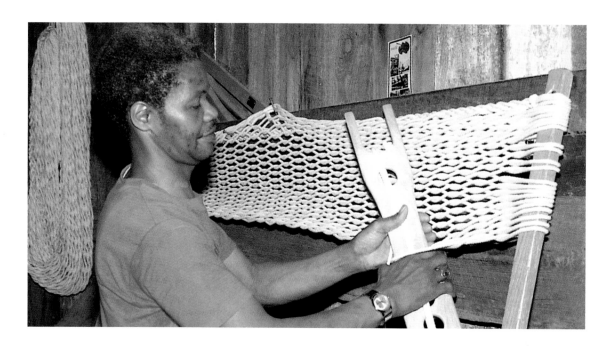

South Carolinians make fishing nets *(above)* and sell handmade pottery *(opposite page)*. Crafts and traditions from many cultures have been passed down through generations.

Most of the people who live in South Carolina were born in South Carolina. Many of them come from families that have lived in the area since colonial days. Two out of three South Carolinians have European ancestors.

African Americans make up slightly less than one-third of the population. Along the southeastern coast, some of them speak a language called **Gullah**—a mixture of African languages, colonial English, and modern American English. Many of the state's 13,000 American Indians are Catawba. Small numbers of Hispanics and Asians make up the rest of the state's population.

History surrounds South Carolinians. Revolutionary battles were fought at a number of sites, including Cowpens and Kings Mountain. At Fort Sumter, visitors can imagine hearing the sounds of the first shots of the Civil War. Old buildings, houses, and plantations are scattered throughout the state.

The Charleston Museum, one of the oldest museums in the United States, displays colonial tools and homes. The South Carolina State Museum in Columbia traces South Carolina's history. Other museums in the state teach about everything from gospel music to military missiles.

The Mountain Dew
Southern 500
takes place on
Labor Day weekend
every year at the
Darlington Raceway.

One of the most famous museums is the Joe Weatherly Museum near the Stock Car Hall of Fame in Darlington. Thousands of people visit this museum when they come to the Mountain Dew Southern 500 stock car race on Labor Day weekend. Other sports fans in South Carolina cheer on the Clemson Tigers and the University of South Carolina's Gamecocks, college sports teams.

South Carolina's beaches and mountains also make the state a fun place to be. People enjoy swimming, boating, and tennis, especially at seaside resorts such as Hilton Head. This island off the Atlantic coast has everything from nature walks to championship golf courses. On the other side of the state, hiking in the Blue Ridge Mountains is a popular activity.

Hilton Head Island draws thousands of tourists to South Carolina every year.

Tourism is a steady source of money and jobs for the state. People who work in the tourist business—in restaurants or hotels, for example—have service jobs. Other kinds of service workers sell food, fabric, or clothing. Columbia and Charleston are important trading centers. More than half of all South Carolinians hold service jobs.

South Carolina's cities hold many
factories and processing plants *(below)*.

South Carolina is home to several military bases.
These soldiers *(above)* are stationed at Fort
Jackson in Columbia.

Many other South Carolinians hold government
jobs. They work for schools, state offices, and the
military. Parris Island, located at the southern end
of the state's coast, has the country's largest train-
ing base for the U.S. Marines. Charleston has both
a naval and an air force base.

About one in six South Carolinians hold manufacturing jobs, many in the textile industry. Most textile mills are in the Up Country. Mill workers make

South Carolina farmers grow peaches *(left)*, soybeans *(below)*, and other crops.

about $2 billion worth of cotton, silk, wool, and other fabrics each year. Other factory workers make fertilizers, chemicals, and paper.

Agriculture is no longer a big business in South Carolina. It accounts for only 2 percent of the state's money and employs only 3 percent of the state's workers, mostly in the Low Country. Cotton is still grown, but tobacco is the state's largest crop. South Carolina is a leading producer of peaches. Soybeans and corn are also major crops. Most livestock farmers raise cows or chickens.

Some South Carolinians mine kaolin, a chalky kind of white clay.

The earth beneath South Carolina's plains and mountains provides jobs, too. Miners cut limestone from the Low Country and carve slabs of granite from the Up Country. Both limestone and granite are used to make roads and buildings. Kaolin, a chalky white clay, and marl, a crumbly substance used in cement and fertilizer, are some of the state's other minerals.

Shrimp make up a big share of South Carolina's seafood industry. Shrimp are the most valuable part of the state's fishing catch, which also includes crabs, oysters, and clams.

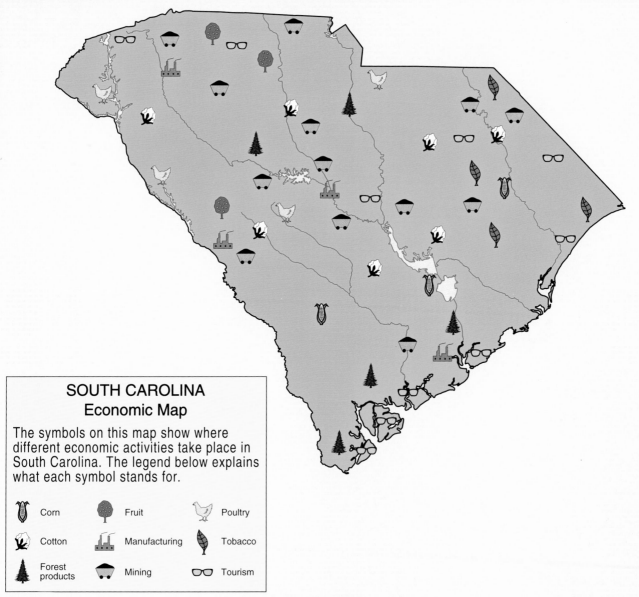

# SOUTH CAROLINA
## Economic Map

The symbols on this map show where different economic activities take place in South Carolina. The legend below explains what each symbol stands for.

| | | | | | |
|---|---|---|---|---|---|
| Corn | | Fruit | | Poultry | |
| Cotton | | Manufacturing | | Tobacco | |
| Forest products | | Mining | | Tourism | |

South Carolina is not the same as it was 200 years ago. What was once an Indian village or a cotton plantation may be the site of a modern mill or factory. But the beauty of the state remains. From the mountain waterfalls of the Up Country to the wide, white beaches of the Low Country, South Carolina remains a jewel of the South.

Some South Carolinians earn their living by commercial fishing.

## Saving the Loggerhead Turtle

On summer nights, huge sea turtles crawl out of the Atlantic Ocean onto South Carolina's beaches. The turtles use their flippers to dig nests in the sand, where each one lays 35 to 180 eggs. Minutes later, the turtles cover their eggs with sand and crawl back to the sea.

Loggerhead turtle

Loggerhead turtles lay eggs on sandy beaches.

The turtles are called loggerheads. The biggest loggerheads can weigh as much as 400 pounds, but their eggs are smaller than Ping-Pong balls. Eight weeks after the eggs are laid, tiny baby turtles, called hatchlings, dig themselves out of their buried nests.

This loggerhead hatchling has wiggled out of its shell and is ready to crawl to the ocean.

The first few days of a loggerhead's life are filled with danger. Seagulls, raccoons, dogs, and ghost crabs like to eat the hatchlings. Even if they don't get eaten, the hatchlings will dry up and die unless they find water. To survive, they must crawl quickly from their nests to the protection of the ocean.

For centuries the young turtles have left their nests at night (when most birds do not hunt) and have easily found the water. Scientists believe that light reflecting off the ocean at night helps guide hatchlings to the water. But in recent years, fewer loggerhead hatchlings have survived the crawl to the ocean.

More and more people have built homes close to South Carolina's beaches. More and more tourists visit the seashore each year. More people means that more cars and other vehicles drive across the sand.  More lights shine on the beach.

   Near resorts and towns, some turtles get
confused by all the streetlights and headlights.
They crawl toward these lights instead of the light
of the ocean.  The hatchlings end up on roads or
highways, where they are often
crushed by oncoming traffic.
Others aren't sure which way
to go.  They wander on the
beach until they are eaten or
until they dry up and die.

Human activity has made
it hard for loggerheads
to reach the sea.

Trucks and cars pack down the sand on beaches. Loggerheads can't dig nests into the packed-down sand.

When people drive cars on the beach, they may unknowingly kill turtles even before they hatch. Cars pack down the sand, making it hard. Oxygen, which the turtle eggs need to develop, cannot always pass through the hardened sand. Eggs that don't get enough oxygen will not hatch. Even if the eggs do hatch, not all hatchlings can dig through the hardened sand, and they die in their nests.

In packed sand, female turtles may not be able to dig nests deep enough to protect their eggs. Hard sand may even keep females from digging nests at all. The turtles may return to the ocean without laying any eggs.

Scientists call problems like the ones facing logger-heads "loss of habitat." Because the turtles are losing their habitat, fewer and fewer loggerheads live along the coast of South Carolina. The population of loggerheads has dropped so much that both South Carolina and the U.S. government have added the animal to the threatened species list. This means that if the turtles aren't protected, their numbers will continue to decrease, and they might die out altogether.

Scientists who have studied loggerhead turtles have ideas about how to help more hatchlings sur-vive the crawl to the ocean. Trapping the animals that eat the hatchlings can save many young tur-tles. Putting wire screens around the nests to pre-vent predators from eating the eggs can also help.

Volunteers track numbers of loggerheads by counting empty eggshells on the beach.

Some scientists think the problems caused by packed sand and streetlights can be solved by carefully moving turtle nests away from the beaches that people use. In addition, streetlights can be shaded by plants, fences, or other barriers to keep artificial light from reaching the beach.

In 1998 scientists at South Carolina's Cape Romain National Wildlife Refuge fitted five loggerhead turtles with tiny satellite transmitters. The transmitters allowed the scientists to track the turtles' movements on land and at sea. Scientists hope that by learning more about how turtles live and travel, they can figure out better ways to protect them.

# ALL ABOUT SOUTH CAROLINA

## Fun Facts

The longest sand sculpture in the world was built in 1990 at Myrtle Beach. Created by 1,613 people, the sculpture stretched more than 10 miles!

In 1890 a South Carolinian started the first commercial tea farm in the United States, American Classic Tea.

The bones of the largest seabird ever known were found near Charleston, South Carolina, in 1984. The bird, which lived about 30 million years ago, is called a pseudodontorn, or bony-toothed bird. It probably weighed 100 pounds and could spread its wings 18 feet wide.

On Christmas Day 1830, the first working steam locomotive built in the United States, named the Best Friend of Charleston, chugged out of Charleston with 141 passengers. That trip began the first regular railroad passenger service in the country.

Main Street in the town of Greenwood, South Carolina, is 350 feet wide. It is the widest main street in the world.

More than forty Hollywood movies have been filmed in South Carolina. They include *The Big Chill, Days of Thunder,* and *Forrest Gump.*

On a hike in South Carolina, you may discover one of the state's 43 kinds of snakes slithering across the trail. Most of these snakes are harmless, but some—including the rattlesnake, copperhead, and coral snake—have poisonous bites.

*Opposite page:* The longest sand sculpture in the world, at Myrtle Beach
*Above:* Brown water snake

# STATE SONG

South Carolina's state song was adopted in 1911. The song's lyrics come from a poem by Henry Timrod, a well-known South Carolina poet.

## CAROLINA

*Words by Henry Timrod; music by Anne C. Burgess*

The des-pot treads thy sa-cred sands, Thy pines give shel - ter to his bands, Thy sons stand by with i - dle hands, Car - o - lin - a, Car - o - lin - a! He breathes at ease thy airs of balm, He scorns the lan - ces of thy palm; Oh, who shall break thy cra-ven calm, Car - o - lin-a, Car - o - lin - a! Thy an - cient fame is grow - ing dim, A spot is on thy gar - ment's rim; Give to the winds thy bat - tle hymn, Car - o - lin - a, Car - o - lin - a!

# A SOUTH CAROLINA RECIPE

African slaves introduced many new foods to the southern United States, including benne, or sesame seeds. Benne cookies are a South Carolina favorite.

## BENNE COOKIES

1 cup benne (sesame) seeds
1½ cups brown sugar, packed
1 cup all-purpose flour
¼ teaspoon baking powder

¼ teaspoon salt
¾ cups butter or margarine, melted
1 egg
1 teaspoon vanilla

1. Ask an adult to help you pre-heat oven to 375° F.
2. Place the benne seeds on an ungreased baking sheet. With an adult's help, toast the seeds in the oven for about 10 to 12 minutes, until they are light brown. Be careful not to let the seeds burn.
3. Mix the toasted seeds and other ingredients in a large bowl.
4. Drop the dough by half teaspoonfuls, 1½ inches apart, onto a greased baking sheet.
5. With an adult's help, bake the cookies for about 4 to 6 minutes, until they're light brown.
6. Let the cookies cool on the baking sheet for about two minutes.
7. Transfer the cookies onto a wire rack to cool completely.
8. Store the cooled cookies in a tightly covered cookie tin.

Makes about six dozen cookies.

# HISTORICAL TIMELINE

**10,000 B.C.**    Native Americans enter the area that later became South Carolina.

**A.D. 1521**    Spaniards reach the Carolina coast.

**1670**    The British build a settlement at Albemarle Point.

**1715**    Settlers and Indians fight the Yamasee War, which lasts about two years.

**1775**    South Carolina joins 12 other colonies in the fight for independence from Britain.

**1776**    Colonel William Moultrie successfully defends a fort on Sullivan's Island against a British attack.

**1780**    American forces defeat the British at the Battle of Kings Mountain.

**1781**    American forces defeat the British at the Battle of Cowpens.

**1788**    South Carolina becomes the eighth state to join the Union.

**1790**    Columbia becomes South Carolina's capital city.

**1860**  South Carolina withdraws from the Union.

**1861**  Confederate troops fire on Fort Sumter in Charleston, starting the Civil War.

**1868**  A new state constitution gives black men the right to vote; South Carolina is allowed to rejoin the United States.

**1891**  The U.S. Marines build a post at Parris Island.

**1922**  Boll weevils destroy about half of South Carolina's cotton crop.

**1941**  A canal and hydroelectric dam are completed between the Santee and Cooper Rivers.

**1983**  I. DeQuincey Newman, the first black state senator since 1888, takes office.

**1989**  Hurricane Hugo damages South Carolina's coast.

**1995**  The Citadel, a public military college in Charleston, admits its first female student.

**2000**  The Confederate flag is removed from atop the South Carolina statehouse.

# OUTSTANDING SOUTH CAROLINIANS

*Mary McLeod Bethune*

**Mary McLeod Bethune** (1875–1955), an educator, grew up in Mayesville, South Carolina. She moved to Florida and started a school for young black women, which later became Bethune-Cookman College. She was president of the college for 20 years.

**Alice Childress** (1920–1994) was born in Charleston but moved, as a young girl, to New York City. An actor, director, and playwright, she also wrote award-winning books for children and young adults, including *A Hero Ain't Nothin' but a Sandwich* (1973).

*May Craig*

**May Craig** (1889–1975), born in Coosaw, South Carolina, was a journalist at a time when the field was dominated by men. Her newspaper articles and radio broadcasts focused on laws that affected women. During World War II (1939–1945), Craig reported from the front lines of battle in France and Germany.

**Beth Daniel** (born 1956), a native of Charleston, is a player on the Ladies Professional Golf Association tour. Since joining the tour in 1979, she has had 32 victories. She ranks third in total winnings for female golfers.

*Stanley Donen*

**Stanley Donen** (born 1924) worked as a film director and choreographer. He is best known for directing classic movie musicals such as *Singin' in the Rain* (1952) and *On the Town* (1949). Donen was born in Columbia and attended the University of South Carolina.

**Joe Frazier** (born 1944) is known as Smokin' Joe in the boxing world. Born in Beaufort, South Carolina, Frazier won an Olympic gold medal in 1964 and was the professional heavyweight champion from 1970 to 1973.

*Joe Frazier*

**Althea Gibson** (born 1927), born in Silver, South Carolina, won the women's singles title at both Wimbledon and the U.S. National Championships in 1957 and 1958. She was the first black woman to win either of these tournaments.

**Dizzy Gillespie**

**John Birks ("Dizzy") Gillespie** (1917–1993) was a trumpet player, composer, and bandleader. In the 1940s, he helped to create a lively, fast-paced style of jazz called bebop. Gillespie was born in Cheraw, South Carolina.

**Angelina Emily Grimké** (1805–1879) and **Sarah Moore Grimké** (1792–1873) were born in Charleston. The Grimké sisters worked to end slavery and to gain rights for women. They were among the first women in the country to give public speeches.

**Wade Hampton**

**Wade Hampton** (1818–1902), born in Charleston, led Confederate soldiers in the Civil War. He became governor of South Carolina in 1876 and worked to make the state's government fair. He appointed black people to state offices and supported voting rights for black men.

**DuBose Heyward** (1885–1940), born in Charleston, wrote poetry and novels about South Carolina's black people. His novel *Porgy* was made into the opera *Porgy and Bess.* Heyward also wrote *Mamba's Daughter* and *Jasbo Brown and Selected Poems.*

**DuBose Heyward**

**Ernest Frederick Hollings** (born 1922) is from Charleston. A U.S. senator since 1966, Hollings has pushed for laws to protect wildlife and the environment. He served as South Carolina's governor from 1959 to 1963.

**Ernest Hollings**

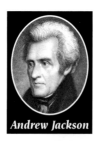

*Andrew Jackson*

**Andrew Jackson** (1767–1845), born in Waxhaw, South Carolina, fought in the Revolutionary War when he was 13. He served as the seventh president of the United States from 1829 to 1837.

**Jesse Jackson** (born 1941), from Greenville, South Carolina, is a Baptist minister and a civil rights leader. Jackson tried to become the Democratic nominee for U.S. president in 1984 and 1988. In 1996, Jackson became president of the Rainbow PUSH Coalition, a social change organization that fights on behalf of workers, women, and people of color.

*Jesse Jackson*

**Ernest Just** (1883–1941) was born in Charleston. In 1915, Just, a biologist who studied cell life, received the first Spingarn Medal, an award for excellence given yearly to a black American.

**Eartha Kitt** (born 1928) is an acclaimed singer, actor, and dancer. She was born in the town of North, South Carolina, and moved to Harlem, New York, as a child. After performing with the Katherine Dunham Dance Group in 1948, she went on to star in films, Broadway shows, and nightclub acts. Kitt is best known for her sultry singing voice.

*Francis Marion*

**Francis Marion** (1732?–1795), nicknamed the Swamp Fox, was a commander during the American Revolution. Born and raised in Berkeley County, South Carolina, he used his knowledge of the state's marshes to fight the British forces.

**Ronald McNair** (1950–1986) grew up in Lake City, South Carolina. An astronaut, he was the second black man to travel in space. McNair was killed when the space shuttle *Challenger* exploded on January 28, 1986.

*Ronald McNair*

**Joseph Hayne Rainey** (1832–1887), a former slave and barber, was the first black man to serve in the U.S. House of Representatives. Born in Georgetown, South Carolina, Rainey was a representative from 1870 to 1879.

*Joseph Rainey*

**Robert Smalls** (1839–1915) was born a slave in Beaufort, South Carolina. During the Civil War, the Confederacy forced Smalls to pilot a ship. One night, he took command of the ship, sailed it into Union hands, and became a Union hero. After the war, Smalls represented South Carolina in both the state and the U.S. legislatures.

*Robert Smalls*

**Strom Thurmond** (born 1902), a Republican U.S. senator, is known for his strong support of states' rights. Born in Edgefield, South Carolina, Thurmond holds records as the oldest person ever to serve in the Senate and for the longest service in the Senate.

**Charles Hard Townes** (born 1915) grew up outside Greenville, South Carolina. Townes and another American scientist introduced the ideas that led to the invention of the laser. This powerful light beam can be used in many ways, such as cutting steel and reading bar codes at the grocery store. Townes won the 1964 Nobel Prize in physics for his work.

*Charles Townes*

# FACTS-AT-A-GLANCE

**Nickname:** Palmetto State

**Song:** "Carolina"

**Mottoes:** *Animis Opibusque Parati* (Prepared in Mind and Resources) and *Dum Spiro Spero* (While I Breathe, I Hope)

**Flower:** yellow jessamine

**Tree:** palmetto

**Bird:** Carolina wren

**Animal:** white-tailed deer

**Insect:** Carolina mantid (praying mantis)

**Fruit:** peach

**Date and ranking of statehood:** May 23, 1788, the eighth state

**Capital:** Columbia

**Area:** 30,111 square miles

**Rank in area, nationwide:** 40th

**Average January temperature:** 45° F

**Average July temperature:** 80° F

Colonel William Moultrie designed South Carolina's flag during the American Revolution. He chose blue to match the color of the uniforms of South Carolina's soldiers. The crescent was the emblem on the soldiers' caps. The palmetto tree was added later. It represents Moultrie's defense of a palmetto log fort on Sullivan's Island against a British attack in 1776.

## POPULATION GROWTH

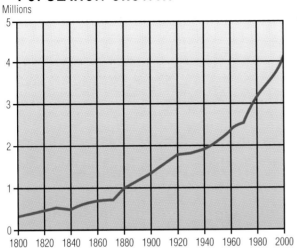

Millions

This chart shows how South Carolina's population has grown from 1800 to 2000.

South Carolina's state seal shows two different scenes. On the left, a palmetto tree above a dead oak tree symbolizes the palmetto log fort on Sullivan's Island that withstood an attack by Britain's oaken ships. On the right, a woman walking on a sword-covered beach represents hope overcoming danger.

**Population:** 4,012,012 (2000 census)

**Rank in population, nationwide:** 26th

**Major cities and populations:** (2000 census) Columbia (116,278), Charleston (96,650), North Charleston (79,641), Greenville (56,002), Rock Hill (49,765)

**U.S. senators:** 2

**U.S. representatives:** 6

**Electoral votes:** 8

**Natural resources:** clay, gold, granite, kaolin, limestone, lumber, marl, peat, sand and gravel, soil, water

**Agricultural products:** beef cattle, chickens, corn, cotton, eggs, hogs, nursery products, peaches, soybeans, tobacco

**Fishing industry:** clams, crabs, finfish, oysters, shrimp

**Manufactured goods:** chemicals, clothing, machinery, paper products, plastic products, rubber products, textiles

## WHERE SOUTH CAROLINIANS WORK

**Services**—57 percent (services include jobs in trade; community, social, and personal services; finance, insurance, and real estate; transportation, communication, and utilities)

**Manufacturing**—17 percent

**Government**—17 percent

**Construction**—6 percent

**Agriculture**—3 percent

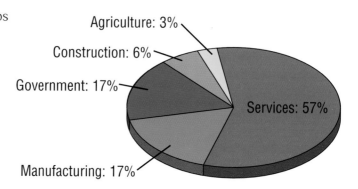

Agriculture: 3%
Construction: 6%
Government: 17%
Services: 57%
Manufacturing: 17%

## GROSS STATE PRODUCT

**Services**—52 percent

**Manufacturing**—26 percent

**Government**—15 percent

**Construction**—5 percent

**Agriculture**—2 percent

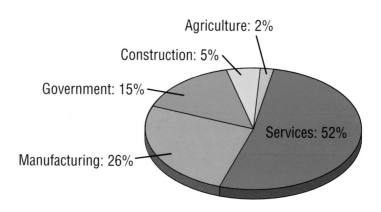

Agriculture: 2%
Construction: 5%
Government: 15%
Services: 52%
Manufacturing: 26%

# SOUTH CAROLINA WILDLIFE

**Mammals:** black bear, bottle-nosed dolphin, cottontail rabbit, fox, fox squirrel, opossum, raccoon, sperm whale, white-tailed deer, wildcat

**Birds:** Carolina wren, duck, mourning dove, quail, wild turkey

**Amphibians and reptiles:** alligator, giant sea turtle, loggerhead turtle, spotted salamander

**Fish:** bass, bream, rockfish, trout

**Trees:** beech, cottonwood, cypress, hemlock, hickory, magnolia, maple, oak, pine, sweet gum, tulip

**Wild plants:** azalea, dwarf white honey-suckle, mountain laurel, palmetto, rhododendron, Spanish moss, sweet bay, Venus's-flytrap, yellow jessamine, yucca

Racoons make their homes in South Carolina's countryside.

# PLACES TO VISIT

**Charles Towne Landing, near Charleston**
The site of the first permanent English settlement in South Carolina, this park includes the original 1670 fort, a replica of a trading ship from the 1600s, and a re-created early South Carolina village.

**Cowpens National Battlefield, Gaffney**
At this site on January 17, 1781, Virginian Daniel Morgan and his troops defeated an elite corps of British redcoats.

**Cypress Gardens, near Charleston**
Visitors can walk and paddle boats through this 163-acre swamp filled with cypress trees, azaleas, camellias, and other trees and flowers.

**Fort Sumter National Monument, Charleston**
The first shots of the Civil War were fired here on April 12, 1861. Visitors can view the fort buildings, learn about the events of April 12, and tour a small museum.

**Stock Car Hall of Fame, Darlington**
Located next to the Darlington Raceway, this site holds the largest collection of stock cars in the world.

**Low Country Legends Music Hall, Charleston**
Visitors can learn about Low Country and Gullah culture here by listening to legends, spirituals, and stories.

**Myrtle Beach, east central South Carolina**
This semitropical resort town is a favorite place for swimming, golfing, fishing, and other outdoor fun.

**Old Exchange and Provost Dungeon, Charleston**
This important Charleston landmark has housed pirates, prisoners, patriots, and presidents during its 300-year history.

**Swan Lake Iris Gardens, Sumter**
All eight species of the world's swans live here in Swan Lake. Japanese irises, camellias, azaleas, and magnolias grow around the lake's dark waters.

**Whitewater Falls, above Salem**
This site contains two waterfalls, each plunging more than 400 feet. The boundary separating North and South Carolina runs between the two falls.

The Cypress Gardens outside of Charleston offer a glimpse into the unusual ecosystem created by water-loving cypress trees.

# ANNUAL EVENTS

Battle of Cowpens Anniversary Celebration, Chesnee—*January*

Myrtle Beach Marathon, Myrtle Beach—*February*

Springfest on Hilton Head Island—*March*

Governor's Frog Jump, Springfield—*April*

Gullah Festival, Beaufort—*May*

Mighty Moo Festival, Cowpens—*June*

South Carolina Peach Festival, Gaffney—*July*

Blue and Gray Encampment, Georgetown—*August*

South Carolina State Fair, Columbia—*October*

Chitlin Strut, Salley—*November*

Christmas on the Farm, Blacksburg—*December*

# LEARN MORE ABOUT SOUTH CAROLINA

## BOOKS

### General

Hoffman, Nancy. *South Carolina.* Tarrytown, NY: Marshall Cavendish, 2000. For older readers.

Stein, R. Conrad. *South Carolina.* New York: Children's Press, 1999.

Thompson, Kathleen. *South Carolina.* New York: Raintree Steck-Vaughn, 1996.

### Special Interest

Colbert, Nancy A. *The Firing on Fort Sumter: A Splintered Nation Goes to War.* Greensboro, NC: Morgan Reynolds, 2001. For older readers. Colbert explores the decisions that led up to the firing on Fort Sumter—the opening shots of the Civil War.

Cornelius, Kay, and Arthur Meier Schlesinger. *Francis Marion: The Swamp Fox.* New York: Chelsea House Publishing, 2000. This biography examines the life of Francis Marion, whose guerilla tactics during the American Revolution earned him the nickname the Swamp Fox.

Lyons, Mary E. *Catching the Fire: Philip Simmons, Blacksmith.* Boston: Houghton Mifflin, 1997. Blacksmith Philip Simmons's elaborate gates, fences, and other ironwork can be seen throughout Charleston. This book tells his story and shows him at work.

McPherson, Stephanie Sammartino. *Sisters Against Slavery: A Story about Sarah and Angelina Grimké.* Minneapolis: Lerner Publications Company, 1999. Daughters of wealthy South Carolina slave owners, the Grimké sisters went on to fight against slavery and to work for women's rights.

## Fiction

Clary, Margie Willis. *A Sweet, Sweet Basket.* Orangeburg, SC: Sandlapper Publishing Company, 1995. By teaching her grandchildren to weave sweet grass baskets, a grandmother passes on her South Carolina and African American heritage.

McGill, Alice. *Miles' Song.* Boston: Houghton Mifflin, 2000. Miles is a 12-year-old slave in South Carolina. When his master sends him to a "breaking ground" for troublemaking slaves, he maintains his spirit by secretly learning to read.

Rinaldi, Ann. *Cast Two Shadows: The American Revolution in the South.* San Diego: Harcourt, 2000. A young girl living in South Carolina during the American Revolution finds her family torn apart by war.

# WEBSITES

**My SCGov.com**, **The Official Website of South Carolina**
<http://www.myscgov.com/>
South Carolina's official website includes news and information on
state government, education, business, health and safety, tourism,
the environment, and more.

**South Carolina: Smiling Faces, Beautiful Places**
<http://www.discoversouthcarolina.com>
Produced by the South Carolina Department of Parks, Recreation,
and Tourism, this site includes everything the traveler needs to
plan a South Carolina vacation, including information on events,
attractions, lodging, and tours.

**The State**
<http://web.thestate.com/content/columbia/front>
South Carolina's largest newspaper, *The State* is the daily paper
from Columbia, the capital city.  It carries local, national, and
international coverage.

**South Carolina State Museum**
<http://www.museum.state.sc.us/>
The acclaimed museum sheds lights on South Carolina's art,
history, natural world, science, and technology.  The website
provides an introduction to the museum's exhibits and programs.

# PRONUNCIATION GUIDE

**Albemarle** (AL-buh-mahrl)

**Catawba** (kuh-TAW-buh)

**Cherokee** (CHEHR-uh-kee)

**Confederate** (kuhn-FEHD-uh-ruht)

**Congaree** (KAHNG-guh-ree)

**Cowpens** (KOW-PEHNZ)

**Edisto** (EHD-uh-stoh)

**Gullah** (GUHL-uh)

**Piedmont** (PEED-mahnt)

**Saluda** (suh-LOOD-uh)

**Santee** (SAN-TEE)

**Sassafras** (SAS-uh-fras)

**Wateree** (WAWT-uh-ree)

**Yamasee** (YAH-muh-see)

Table Rock State Park

# GLOSSARY

**civil rights movement:** a movement to gain equal rights, or freedoms, for all citizens—regardless of race, religion, or sex

**colony:** a territory ruled by a country some distance away

**Gullah:** the language spoken by a group of black people living along the coast and on the Sea Islands of the southeastern United States. Gullah is a combination of English and several African languages.

**hydropower:** electricity produced by waterpower; also called hydroelectric power

**Jim Crow laws:** measures that separated black people from white people in public places, such as schools, parks, theaters, and restaurants. Jim Crow laws were enforced in the U.S. South from 1877 to the 1950s.

**Reconstruction:** the period from 1865 to 1877, during which the U.S. government rebuilt Southern cities and businesses that had been destroyed during the Civil War. During this period, the government also determined how to bring the Southern states back into the Union.

**secede:** to stop being a member of a political union or other group

**sharecropper:** a person who farms land that belongs to someone else. As payment for their labor, sharecroppers get houses, tools, and a share of the crops they grow.

**swamp:** a wetland permanently soaked with water. Woody plants (trees and shrubs) are the main form of vegetation there.

**tariff:** a tax charged by a government on goods bought from or sold to other countries

# INDEX

# PHOTO ACKNOWLEDGMENTS

Cover Photographs by © Neil Rabinowitz/CORBIS, © Bill Ross/CORBIS; PresentationMaps.com, pp. 1, 8, 9, 49; © David Muench/CORBIS, pp. 2–3; © Michael T. Sedam/CORBIS, p. 3; © Pat O'Hara/CORBIS, pp. (detail) 4, (detail) 7, (detail) 16, (detail) 40, (detail) 52; © Annie Griffiths Belt/CORBIS, p. 6; South Carolina Department of Parks, Recreation, and Tourism, pp. 7, 53, 75, 80; © Jay Browne, S.C. Forestry Commission, pp. 10, 11, 12, 13; Olde English District Commission, p. 14 (top); © JeffGreenberg@juno.com, p. 14 (center); © Cabisco/Visuals Unlimited, p. 14 (bottom); Tom J. Ulrich/Visuals Unlimited, p. 15; Library of Congress, pp. 16, 26, 27, 28, 32, 67 (second from top), 68 (top, second from bottom), 69 (top, bottom); From the Collection of the South Carolina State Museum, p. 17; Joanna Angle, pp. 18, 43; By permission of the British Library, p. 19; From the Collections of the South Carolina Historical Society, pp. 20, 23; The South Caroliniana Library, University of South Carolina, pp. 21, 22, 24, 30, 31, 33, 34, 35, 67 (second from bottom), 69 (center), 70 (bottom); Independent Picture Service, pp. 25, 66 (bottom), 67 (second from top); © CORBIS, p. 29; Bettmann/CORBIS pp. 37, 66 (second from bottom), 68 (second from bottom); © Tina Manley, p. 38; © Richard Bickel/CORBIS, p. 41; Doyen Salsig, p. 42; © ALLSPORT USA/Chris Stanford, p. 44; © Marion Culp/Visuals Unlimited, p. 45; U.S. Army Ft. Jackson, p. 46 (top left); South Carolina Department of Agriculture, p. 47; J.M. Huber Corporation, Langley, South Carolina, p. 48; © Joseph L. Fontenot/Visuals Unlimited, p. 51; © David S. Addison/Visuals Unlimited, p. 54; © Lynn Stone, pp. 55, 58; Larry Cameron, Coastal Science Engineering, Inc., p. 56; © Joel Arrington/Visuals Unlimited, p. 59; Myrtle Beach Chamber of Commerce, p. 60; © David Dvorak Jr., p. 61; Hollywood Book and Poster, p. 67 (top); National Archives, pp. 66 (second from top), 67 (bottom); © Reuters NewMedia Inc./CORBIS, p. 68 (second from top); Columbia University, p. 69 (center); Jean Matheny, p. 70 (top); © Raymond Gehman/CORBIS, p. 73